BASICS OF
STOCK MARKET

INDEX

1. INTRODUCTION TO THE STOCK MARKET........................ 3-7

2. HISTORY OF INDIAN STOCK MARKET...............................8-12

3. HOW THE INDIAN STOCK MARKET WORKS..................13-17

4. REGULATIONS OF INDIAN STOCK MARKET...................18-23

5. HOW TO START INVESTING IN THE STOCK MARKET..24-28

6. TYPES OF INVESTMENTS..29-35

7. ANALYSING STOCKS:FUNDAMENTAL...........................

AND TECHNICAL ANALYSIS..36-42

8. RISKS AND REWARDS IN STOCK MARKET.....................43-48

9. STRATEGIES FOR LONG TERM SUCCESS........................49-54

10. BUILDING AND MANAGING A BALANCED PORTFOLIO..55-60

11. ANALYSING MARKET TRENDS AND ECONOMIC INDICATORS..61-66

12. PSYCHOLOGY OF INVESTING...67-71

13. BUILDING A LONG TERM INVESTMENT 72-76

14. ROLE OF TECHNOLOGY IN MODERN INVESTING.......77-80

15. COMMON MISTAKES TO AVOID IN INVESTING..........81-86

Chapter 1: Introduction to the Stock Market

What is a Stock Market?

The stock market is a well-structured platform where shares of companies are issued and traded, either through exchanges or over-the-counter markets. It is a vital component of the financial ecosystem, providing a marketplace where companies raise capital by issuing ownership shares, and investors buy those shares to become part-owners.

In simpler terms, think of the stock market as a supermarket for financial securities like stocks, bonds, and mutual funds. Just as shoppers buy groceries in a supermarket, investors buy and sell shares in the stock market.

Primary Market: This is where companies issue new shares through Initial Public Offerings (IPOs) to raise funds.

Secondary Market: Once shares are issued in the primary market, they are traded among investors in the secondary market.

For example, if Infosys wants to expand its operations, it can raise money by offering its shares to the public through an IPO. After the IPO, these shares can be bought or sold on stock exchanges like the NSE or BSE.

Importance of the Stock Market

The stock market holds significant importance not just for investors but also for businesses and the economy at large. Below are some of its key benefits:

Facilitates Capital Formation:

By allowing companies to raise funds, the stock market supports the expansion of industries and infrastructure. This ultimately boosts economic productivity.

Enables Wealth Creation:

Investors can grow their wealth by investing in the stock market, especially over the long term. Historically, stocks have provided higher returns compared to traditional investment options like savings accounts or fixed deposits. For instance, the Sensex, the benchmark index of the Bombay Stock Exchange (BSE), has delivered significant returns to investors over decades.

Promotes Economic Efficiency:

Companies that perform well attract more investment. This ensures that resources flow to the most efficient and profitable businesses, driving innovation and competition.

Improves Financial Literacy and Planning:

Participation in the stock market encourages individuals to learn about economic trends, corporate performance, and global markets, leading to better financial planning.

Liquidity for Investors:

The stock market ensures that investors can easily buy or sell shares at prevailing market prices, making it a liquid investment option. Unlike real estate or fixed deposits, which may take time to liquidate, stocks can be sold almost instantly.

Role of the Stock Market in the Economy

The stock market is often described as the backbone of a nation's financial system. It serves as a key indicator of economic health and facilitates growth by performing the following functions:

Mobilization of Savings into Investments:

Savings sitting idle in bank accounts do not contribute to economic growth. The stock market allows individuals to invest these savings into productive assets, thereby fueling industrial and economic expansion.

Job Creation:

Companies that raise funds through the stock market can expand their operations, leading to more job opportunities.

Global Integration:

In a globalized world, the stock market acts as a bridge connecting domestic businesses with international investors. For instance, foreign institutional investors (FIIs) often invest in Indian companies listed on the NSE or BSE.

Stabilizing the Economy:

A well-regulated stock market, overseen by bodies like SEBI, provides stability by maintaining transparency and protecting investor interests. This reduces systemic risks and promotes trust in the financial system.

Why Should You Understand the Stock Market?

The stock market is not just a domain for seasoned investors or financial experts. It is increasingly becoming a tool for ordinary individuals to achieve their financial goals. Understanding the stock market empowers you to:

Plan for Long-term Goals:

Whether you're saving for your child's education, buying a house, or planning your retirement, the stock market provides opportunities to grow your money over time.

Combat Inflation:

Inflation erodes the purchasing power of money over time. Investments in the stock market typically offer returns that outpace inflation, preserving and increasing your wealth.

Generate Passive Income:

Stocks of profitable companies often pay dividends to shareholders, providing a steady stream of income in addition to capital appreciation.

Take Control of Your Financial Future:

Relying solely on fixed-income instruments or government schemes may not be enough in today's economy. The stock market gives you an active role in managing and growing your wealth.

Common Misconceptions About the Stock Market

Before we dive deeper into the mechanics of the stock market in later chapters, it's essential to address some myths that often discourage people from participating:

"The Stock Market is a Gamble."

While short-term trading can be risky, investing in fundamentally strong companies for the long term is far from gambling. It involves careful analysis and strategic decision-making.

"You Need a Lot of Money to Start."

Today, platforms allow you to invest with as little as ₹100. Systematic Investment Plans (SIPs) in mutual funds are a great way to start small.

"Only Experts Can Make Money."

With the right knowledge and discipline, anyone can succeed in the stock market. Tools, resources, and educational materials are now widely available.

"The Stock Market is Only for the Rich."

On the contrary, the stock market is accessible to people from all walks of life. Demat and trading accounts have made the process user-friendly.

Conclusion

The stock market is an integral part of the financial system, offering opportunities for wealth creation and economic development. Understanding its basics is the first step towards making informed investment decisions and achieving your financial goals.

In the following chapters, we will explore the history of the Indian stock market, key regulatory bodies like SEBI, and how you can start investing step by step.

Chapter 2: History of the Indian Stock Market

The Indian stock market has a rich and storied history that reflects the evolution of India's financial system and economic growth. From its informal beginnings in the 19th century to its transformation into a modern, tech-driven marketplace, the Indian stock market has come a long way. This chapter traces the key milestones in its development, highlighting the pivotal moments and their impact on the economy.

The Beginnings: Informal Trading (1830s - 1870s)

The roots of the Indian stock market can be traced back to the early 1830s during the era of British rule. Informal trading of shares began with a handful of brokers in Mumbai (then Bombay). These brokers would gather under a banyan tree in the city's bustling business district to trade shares of companies like the East India Company.

While this was not a formal market, it laid the foundation for organized trading. The lack of regulations and infrastructure meant that trading was limited to a small group of participants.

The Formation of the Bombay Stock Exchange (BSE) (1875)

In 1875, 22 stockbrokers came together to establish the Native Share and Stock Brokers Association in Bombay, marking the birth of the Bombay Stock Exchange (BSE). This was the first organized stock exchange in Asia and remains one of the oldest in the world.

Key highlights:

The BSE initially operated under a banyan tree before moving to its current location at Dalal Street, Mumbai.

It provided a structured platform for trading, setting the stage for transparency and efficiency.

Post-Independence Developments (1947 - 1980s)

After India gained independence in 1947, the stock market began to grow alongside the country's industrial development. Key events during this period include:

Nationalization of Key Industries (1950s):

The government's focus on public sector undertakings (PSUs) led to the listing of several state-owned enterprises.

Introduction of Regulation (1956):

The Companies Act of 1956 established guidelines for company listings and investor protection, providing a legal framework for the stock market.

Regional Stock Exchanges (1960s-1970s):

Several regional stock exchanges, such as the Calcutta Stock Exchange and Madras Stock Exchange, were established to cater to local investors.

The Advent of NSE and Modernization (1990s)

The liberalization of the Indian economy in 1991 marked a turning point for the stock market. Economic reforms opened the country to foreign investments, and the government introduced several measures to modernize financial markets.

Establishment of the National Stock Exchange (NSE) (1992):

The NSE was introduced as a fully electronic stock exchange to compete with the BSE.

It revolutionized trading by eliminating the traditional open-outcry system and replacing it with a screen-based electronic trading platform.

SEBI's Role:

The Securities and Exchange Board of India (SEBI), established in 1988 and granted statutory powers in 1992, became the primary regulator of the Indian stock market. It ensured transparency, curbed malpractices, and safeguarded investor interests.

Introduction of Demat Accounts (1996):

The transition from physical share certificates to electronic shares through Demat accounts made trading more efficient and secure.

Key Milestones in Recent Decades

Boom of the IT Sector (2000s):

The rapid growth of technology companies like Infosys, Wipro, and TCS boosted investor confidence and attracted foreign institutional investors (FIIs).

Sensex Crosses Major Milestones:

The BSE Sensex, India's benchmark index, crossed the 10,000 mark in 2006 and the 50,000 mark in 2021, reflecting the market's growth and resilience.

Introduction of Derivatives (2000):

The NSE launched derivatives trading, including futures and options, enabling investors to hedge risks and speculate on market movements.

Integration of Global Markets (2008):

The global financial crisis of 2008 impacted the Indian stock market, but its swift recovery highlighted the resilience of Indian companies and the economy.

Digital Revolution (2010s):

The rise of digital trading platforms and mobile apps democratized stock market participation, enabling retail investors to trade with ease.

Inclusion in Global Indices:

Indian companies became part of global indices like the MSCI Emerging Markets Index, attracting international investment.

The Role of Technology and Automation

Technology has played a crucial role in shaping the modern Indian stock market:

Algorithmic Trading: Automated trading strategies execute trades at high speeds and efficiency.

Online Trading Platforms: Apps like Zerodha and Groww have made stock market participation easier for retail investors.

Real-Time Market Data: Investors can access live prices, charts, and financial news, enabling informed decision-making.

Key Challenges Over Time

Despite its growth, the Indian stock market has faced several challenges:

Scams and Fraud:

The Harshad Mehta scam (1992) and Ketan Parekh scam (2001) revealed vulnerabilities in the system.

These incidents led to stricter regulations and reforms.

Market Volatility:

External factors like global crises and internal issues like policy uncertainty often cause sharp fluctuations in the market.

Low Financial Literacy:

A significant portion of the population remains unaware of the benefits and risks of stock market investing.

Conclusion

The history of the Indian stock market is a testament to its evolution from an informal trading hub to a globally recognized marketplace. Today, it stands as a pillar of India's economic strength, offering opportunities for wealth creation and capital formation.

In the next chapter, we will explore how the Indian stock market functions, covering its structure, key participants, and trading mechanisms.

Chapter 3: How the Indian Stock Market Works

Understanding how the Indian stock market functions is key to navigating it effectively. This chapter provides an overview of the stock market's structure, participants, and mechanisms, explaining the process of buying, selling, and trading shares.

Structure of the Indian Stock Market

The Indian stock market is structured into two main categories:

Primary Market:

This is where companies issue new shares to the public through Initial Public Offerings (IPOs).

Investors buy shares directly from the company, which uses the funds for growth, debt repayment, or other corporate purposes.

Example: When Zomato issued its IPO in 2021, investors purchased shares at the offer price directly from the company.

Secondary Market:

Once shares are issued in the primary market, they are traded among investors in the secondary market.

Trades are conducted on stock exchanges like the Bombay Stock Exchange (BSE) and the National Stock Exchange (NSE).

Key Players in the Indian Stock Market

Retail Investors:

Individual investors who trade in smaller quantities compared to institutional investors.

Institutional Investors:

Large entities like mutual funds, pension funds, and foreign institutional investors (FIIs) that trade in significant volumes.

Stockbrokers:

Registered intermediaries who facilitate trading on behalf of investors. Examples include Zerodha, Angel One, and ICICI Direct.

SEBI (Securities and Exchange Board of India):

The regulatory authority that ensures transparency, prevents malpractices, and protects investor interests.

Depositories:

Organizations like NSDL (National Securities Depository Limited) and CDSL (Central Depository Services Limited) that hold securities electronically in Demat accounts.

How Trading Happens

Opening a Demat and Trading Account:

To trade, you need a Demat account (to hold shares in electronic form) and a trading account (to place buy/sell orders).

Placing Orders:

Investors place buy or sell orders through their stockbroker. Orders specify the stock, quantity, and price.

Example: If you want to buy 100 shares of Reliance Industries at ₹2,500 each, you place a "limit order" specifying these details.

Matching of Orders:

Stock exchanges match buy and sell orders based on price and quantity.

Example: If a seller agrees to sell 100 shares of Reliance at ₹2,500, the transaction is executed.

Settlement of Trades:

In India, trades follow a T+1 settlement cycle. If you buy shares today (T), they will be credited to your Demat account the next day (T+1).

Trading Mechanisms

Order Types:

Market Order: Executes the trade at the current market price.

Limit Order: Executes only at the specified price or better.

Trading Hours:

The Indian stock market operates from 9:15 AM to 3:30 PM (Monday to Friday).

Intraday vs Delivery Trading:

Intraday Trading: Buy and sell shares within the same trading day.

Delivery Trading: Hold shares for more than one day.

Derivatives Trading:

Futures and options contracts allow investors to speculate on or hedge against market movements.

The Role of Stock Exchanges

Bombay Stock Exchange (BSE):

Established in 1875, it is Asia's oldest stock exchange.

Known for its benchmark index, the Sensex.

National Stock Exchange (NSE):

Established in 1992, it introduced electronic trading to India.

Known for its benchmark index, the Nifty 50.

Both exchanges play a critical role in ensuring liquidity, transparency, and fair pricing.

Role of SEBI in Market Regulation

SEBI ensures:

Fair practices in trading.

Protection of small investors from fraud.

Monitoring and regulating market participants.

Example: SEBI banned insider trading, ensuring no unfair advantage to those with confidential company information.

Benefits of the Indian Stock Market

Access to Capital for Companies:

Companies can raise funds efficiently, fueling growth and innovation.

Opportunity for Wealth Creation:

Long-term investments in the stock market have historically generated substantial wealth for investors.

Diversification Options:

A wide range of industries and sectors allows for portfolio diversification.

Risks in the Stock Market

Market Volatility:

Prices fluctuate due to factors like economic news, global events, and company performance.

Systematic Risk:

Risks affecting the entire market, such as economic downturns or geopolitical tensions.

Unsystematic Risk:

Risks specific to a company, such as poor management or declining profitability.

Emotional Trading:

Decisions driven by fear or greed often lead to losses.

Conclusion

The Indian stock market is a dynamic ecosystem that facilitates the trading of securities, contributing to wealth creation and economic development. By understanding its structure and functioning, investors can make informed decisions and navigate the complexities of the market effectively.

In the next chapter, we will explore the regulators of the Indian stock market, focusing on SEBI's role in maintaining transparency and fairness

Chapter 4: Regulators of the Indian Stock Market

Regulation is the backbone of any well-functioning stock market. In India, the regulatory framework ensures transparency, fairness, and investor protection while maintaining the integrity of the financial markets. This chapter focuses on the key regulators of the Indian stock market, particularly the Securities and Exchange Board of India (SEBI), with real-life examples to illustrate their roles.

Key Regulators of the Indian Stock Market

Securities and Exchange Board of India (SEBI):

SEBI is the primary regulatory authority for the Indian stock market. Established in 1988 and given statutory powers in 1992, SEBI's primary objective is to protect the interests of investors and ensure the smooth functioning of the stock market.

Stock Exchanges (BSE and NSE):

While primarily trading platforms, stock exchanges also have self-regulatory responsibilities. They monitor listed companies and trading activities to ensure compliance with regulations.

Reserve Bank of India (RBI):

The RBI oversees foreign exchange transactions, monetary policy, and the regulation of banks involved in the stock market.

Ministry of Corporate Affairs (MCA):

The MCA governs corporate laws in India, including the Companies Act, which ensures that companies follow rules related to their financial disclosures and governance.

Depositories (NSDL and CDSL):

These entities manage electronic securities through Demat accounts and ensure the safekeeping of investors' holdings.

Role of SEBI in the Indian Stock Market

1. Protecting Investors

SEBI ensures that investors are not exploited or misled by fraudulent practices.

Example:

In the Harshad Mehta scam (1992), stock prices were artificially inflated using money borrowed from banks. After this scam, SEBI implemented stricter regulations on stock manipulation, ensuring such practices are detected and penalized.

2. Regulating Market Participants

SEBI monitors brokers, mutual funds, portfolio managers, and other entities to ensure they comply with market norms.

Example:

If a broker engages in insider trading (buying or selling shares based on non-public information), SEBI investigates and imposes penalties. For instance, SEBI banned a major brokerage firm in 2020 for such unethical practices.

3. Introducing Reforms

SEBI constantly updates rules to keep up with evolving market needs.

Example:

To protect small investors, SEBI made it mandatory for mutual fund schemes to disclose their risk levels using a "Risk-o-Meter." This helps investors make informed decisions.

4. Ensuring Fair Practices

SEBI ensures that IPOs, rights issues, and other capital-raising activities are conducted transparently.

Example:

In the case of Paytm's IPO in 2021, SEBI reviewed the company's prospectus to ensure all financial details and risks were disclosed to the public before the IPO launch.

Role of Stock Exchanges

Stock exchanges like BSE and NSE play an essential role in ensuring compliance and transparency.

Monitoring Trading Activities:

Exchanges track unusual price movements to identify potential market manipulation.

Example:

If a stock like Adani Enterprises experiences sudden and unexplained price surges, the NSE investigates the trades and asks for clarifications from the company.

Suspension of Non-Compliant Companies:

Companies that fail to comply with listing requirements are delisted or suspended.

Example:

In 2019, the BSE delisted over 200 companies for failing to meet regulatory requirements, ensuring market integrity.

Role of RBI in Stock Market Regulation

The Reserve Bank of India regulates banks and foreign exchange transactions, ensuring stability in the financial markets.

Foreign Institutional Investments (FII):

RBI monitors and regulates the flow of foreign capital into the Indian stock market.

Example:

When foreign investors buy shares of Infosys or HDFC Bank, RBI ensures that the transactions comply with foreign exchange rules.

Monetary Policy:

Changes in interest rates by the RBI directly impact stock market performance.

Example:

If the RBI reduces interest rates, borrowing becomes cheaper for companies, often leading to higher stock prices as businesses expand.

Depositories: NSDL and CDSL

Depositories ensure the safe storage of shares in electronic format and enable smooth settlement of trades.

Holding Shares Electronically:

Investors no longer need physical share certificates, reducing risks like theft or forgery.

Example:

When you buy shares of Tata Steel, they are credited to your Demat account maintained by NSDL or CDSL.

Facilitating Seamless Transfers:

Depositories ensure that shares are transferred smoothly during buy or sell transactions.

Example:

If you sell 50 shares of Reliance Industries, CDSL debits these shares from your account and credits them to the buyer's account.

Ministry of Corporate Affairs (MCA)

The MCA ensures companies follow corporate governance norms and financial transparency.

Example:

In 2018, the MCA investigated a company for falsifying its financial statements, leading to its delisting and criminal charges against its directors.

Notable Regulatory Actions in Indian Stock Market History

Satyam Scandal (2009):

Satyam Computers falsified its financial statements, inflating profits.

SEBI imposed penalties and strengthened corporate governance norms to prevent such incidents.

IL&FS Crisis (2018):

Infrastructure Leasing & Financial Services (IL&FS) defaulted on loans, causing a market panic.

SEBI and RBI intervened to restore investor confidence.

How Regulations Benefit Investors

Enhanced Transparency:

Investors can access accurate and timely information, enabling informed decision-making.

Reduced Fraud:

Regulatory oversight minimizes the risk of scams and unethical practices.

Increased Confidence:

A well-regulated market attracts both domestic and international investors, boosting liquidity and stability.

Conclusion

The regulators of the Indian stock market, led by SEBI, play a crucial role in ensuring its efficiency, transparency, and fairness. By maintaining a robust regulatory framework, they protect investors, promote market integrity, and facilitate economic growth.

In the next chapter, we will explore how to start investing in the Indian stock market, guiding readers through the step-by-step process of becoming a market participant.

Chapter 5: How to Start Investing in the Indian Stock Market

Investing in the stock market can be a transformative financial journey, offering opportunities to grow your wealth and achieve financial independence. However, the process may seem daunting to beginners. This chapter provides a detailed, step-by-step guide to help you start your investment journey confidently.

1. Understand the Basics

Before diving in, familiarize yourself with key stock market concepts:

Shares: Represent ownership in a company. Buying a share makes you a partial owner of the company.

Stock Market Indices: Benchmarks like Sensex and Nifty 50 help track market performance.

Types of Markets:

Primary Market: For IPOs where companies sell shares for the first time.

Secondary Market: For trading already-issued shares.

Example: Suppose Reliance Industries issues new shares in the primary market through an IPO. Once listed, these shares can be bought and sold in the secondary market.

2. Prerequisites for Investing

To invest in the Indian stock market, you need:

PAN Card: A mandatory identification for all financial transactions in India.

Bank Account: To transfer funds for buying stocks and receive dividends.

Demat Account: Holds your securities electronically.

Trading Account: Allows you to buy and sell shares.

Note: Many brokers, like Zerodha or ICICI Direct, offer both Demat and trading accounts as a package.

3. Choosing a Stockbroker

A stockbroker acts as an intermediary between you and the stock exchange. Choose a broker based on:

Brokerage Charges: Discount brokers like Zerodha offer lower fees than full-service brokers like HDFC Securities.

Ease of Use: A user-friendly trading platform is essential for beginners.

Research Tools: Brokers with in-depth analysis tools can help you make informed decisions.

Example: Ramesh, a new investor, opted for Upstox because of its simple interface and low brokerage fees.

4. Open a Demat and Trading Account

The process is straightforward:

Select a broker and visit their website.

Fill out the application form and complete KYC (Know Your Customer) requirements.

Upload necessary documents like PAN, Aadhaar, and bank statements.

After verification, your account will be activated.

Example: Priya opened her Demat account with Angel One and started trading within 3 days.

5. Set Clear Financial Goals

Define your purpose for investing. Are you:

Saving for a short-term goal like a vacation?

Building wealth for long-term goals like retirement?

Looking for passive income through dividends?

Example: Rahul aimed to save ₹5 lakhs in 10 years for his child's education and invested in blue-chip stocks like Infosys and TCS.

6. Research Before Investing

Successful investing requires thorough research:

Study the Company: Analyze the business model, financial performance, and growth prospects.

Understand Market Trends: Stay updated with economic and industry news.

Compare Valuations: Use metrics like the Price-to-Earnings (P/E) ratio to assess whether a stock is overvalued or undervalued.

Example: Before buying HDFC Bank shares, Sunita reviewed its quarterly earnings reports and compared its P/E ratio with peers.

7. Start Small and Diversify

As a beginner, invest small amounts and spread your investments across multiple sectors to reduce risk.

Example: Instead of investing ₹1 lakh entirely in IT stocks, Rohan allocated ₹30,000 to IT, ₹30,000 to FMCG, and ₹40,000 to pharmaceuticals.

8. Place Your First Trade

Once you've chosen a stock:

Log into your trading platform.

Search for the stock you want to buy.

Enter the quantity and price (market or limit order).

Confirm the transaction.

Example: Meera bought 10 shares of Tata Motors at a market price of ₹500 each.

9. Monitor Your Investments

Regularly review your portfolio to ensure it aligns with your financial goals. Avoid frequent trading based on short-term market fluctuations.

Example: Suresh held his shares in ITC for 5 years despite short-term dips, eventually reaping substantial profits.

10. Use Stop-Loss and Target Orders

To manage risk, set:

Stop-Loss Order: Automatically sells the stock if the price falls below a certain level.

Target Order: Automatically sells the stock once it reaches a desired profit level.

Example: Ravi set a stop-loss at ₹900 and a target at ₹1,200 for his HDFC Bank shares, ensuring limited losses and secured profits.

Common Mistakes to Avoid

Investing Without Research: Relying on tips or rumors often leads to losses.

Emotional Trading: Panic selling during market dips can erode your capital.

Overleveraging: Avoid borrowing excessively to invest.

Ignoring Diversification: Concentrating all investments in one sector increases risk.

Example: Arjun lost ₹50,000 in a single trade because he invested heavily in a small-cap stock based on a friend's tip.

Investing for Long-Term Success

Patience is Key: Long-term investments often outperform short-term trades.

Reinvest Dividends: Compounding can significantly boost your returns.

Stay Updated: Follow financial news and updates from companies you've invested in.

Example: Neha invested ₹1 lakh in Asian Paints in 2010 and held her investment for 10 years. The value of her shares grew to over ₹8 lakhs, thanks to consistent growth and reinvested dividends.

Conclusion

Starting your investment journey in the Indian stock market is an empowering step toward financial independence. By following these steps, conducting thorough research, and maintaining discipline, you can navigate the complexities of the stock market and achieve your financial goals.

In the next chapter, we will explore the various types of investments in the Indian stock market to help you diversify and optimize your portfolio.

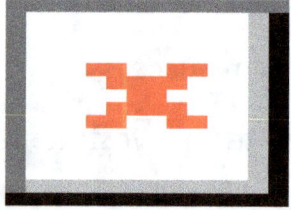

Chapter 6:

Types of Investments in the Indian Stock Market

The Indian stock market offers various investment options, catering to different financial goals, risk appetites, and timelines. This chapter dives into the types of investments available, providing detailed explanations and real-life examples to help you make informed decisions.

1. Equity Shares (Stocks)

Equity shares represent ownership in a company. By buying shares, you become a part-owner and can benefit from the company's growth.

Benefits:

High potential returns.

Dividends (profit-sharing by the company).

Voting rights in company decisions.

Risks:

Market volatility.

Price fluctuations due to external factors.

Example:

Imagine you bought 100 shares of Infosys at ₹1,000 each in 2010. By 2023, the stock price rose to ₹15,000 per share. Your initial investment of ₹1,00,000 would now be worth ₹15,00,000, showcasing the power of equity investments over the long term.

2. Bonds

Bonds are debt instruments issued by companies or governments to raise funds. Investors earn interest (coupon payments) and get the principal amount back at maturity.

Types of Bonds:

Government Bonds: Issued by the government, these are considered risk-free.

Corporate Bonds: Issued by private companies, these carry higher risks but offer better returns.

Benefits:

Fixed and predictable income.

Lower risk compared to equities.

Risks:

Credit risk (issuer default).

Interest rate risk.

Example:

If you buy a government bond for ₹10,000 with a 7% annual return, you'll earn ₹700 yearly, plus your ₹10,000 back at the end of the bond's term.

3. Mutual Funds

Mutual funds pool money from multiple investors and invest in a diversified portfolio of stocks, bonds, or other assets.

Types of Mutual Funds:

Equity Mutual Funds: Invest primarily in stocks.

Debt Mutual Funds: Focus on fixed-income securities like bonds.

Hybrid Funds: A mix of equity and debt for balanced risk and return.

Benefits:

Professionally managed.

Diversification reduces risk.

Risks:

Market-linked returns.

Management fees can reduce profits.

Example:

The SBI Bluechip Fund, an equity mutual fund, has delivered consistent returns over the past decade, making it a popular choice for long-term investors.

4. Exchange-Traded Funds (ETFs)

ETFs are similar to mutual funds but trade like stocks on exchanges. They track indices such as the Nifty 50 or Sensex.

Benefits:

Low expense ratio.

High liquidity.

Transparent pricing.

Risks:

Limited potential for outperforming the market.

Subject to market volatility.

Example:

Investing in a Nifty 50 ETF gives you exposure to India's top 50 companies, providing a diversified and cost-effective investment option.

5. Derivatives

Derivatives are financial instruments whose value is derived from an underlying asset, such as stocks or commodities.

Types:

Futures: Contracts to buy or sell an asset at a predetermined price on a future date.

Options: Contracts giving the right (but not obligation) to buy or sell an asset at a specific price.

Benefits:

Hedging against risks.

High potential for short-term gains.

Risks:

Complex and speculative.

High risk of loss.

Example:

If you expect Reliance Industries' stock to rise, you could buy a call option at ₹2,500. If the price rises to ₹2,700, you profit from the difference.

6. Initial Public Offerings (IPOs)

An IPO allows a company to raise funds by selling its shares to the public for the first time.

Benefits:

Opportunity to invest early in promising companies.

Potential for high returns if the company performs well.

Risks:

Lack of historical performance data.

Overvaluation during IPOs.

Example:

Zomato's IPO in 2021 allowed investors to buy shares at ₹76. Early investors saw significant returns when the stock price surged after listing.

7. Small-Cap, Mid-Cap, and Large-Cap Investments

Large-Cap Stocks:

Established companies with stable returns.

Example: Reliance Industries, HDFC Bank.

Mid-Cap Stocks:

Companies with growth potential but higher risk than large caps.

Example: Tata Chemicals, Bharat Forge.

Small-Cap Stocks:

Emerging companies with high growth potential but significant risks.

Example: Tanla Platforms, Suzlon Energy.

8. Real Estate Investment Trusts (REITs)

REITs pool investor money to invest in income-generating real estate assets like commercial properties.

Benefits:

Regular income through dividends.

Exposure to real estate without owning property.

Risks:

Subject to property market fluctuations.

Example:

Embassy REIT, India's first publicly listed REIT, offers exposure to high-quality office spaces.

9. Gold ETFs and Sovereign Gold Bonds (SGBs)

Gold ETFs: Track gold prices and trade like stocks.

SGBs: Issued by the government, offering fixed interest plus gold price appreciation.

Example:

If you invest in a Gold ETF, you benefit from gold price increases without the hassle of storing physical gold.

10. Fixed Deposits and Recurring Deposits

Although not directly linked to the stock market, these are low-risk investment options for conservative investors.

Benefits:

Guaranteed returns.

Safe for risk-averse investors.

Risks:

Low returns compared to equities.

Conclusion

Understanding the types of investments in the Indian stock market is crucial for building a diversified portfolio. Each option has unique features, benefits, and risks. By aligning your investments with your financial goals, risk tolerance, and investment horizon, you can optimize returns while managing risks effectively.

The next chapter delves into analyzing stocks through fundamental and technical analysis, essential skills for evaluating investment opportunities.

Chapter 7: Analyzing Stocks: Fundamental and Technical Analysis

Before making any investment in the stock market, it's essential to assess whether a stock is a good buy or not. This can be done through two main approaches: Fundamental Analysis and Technical Analysis. Both methods offer valuable insights but focus on different aspects of a stock's performance. In this chapter, we'll explore both in detail, with practical examples to help you understand how to apply them.

1. Fundamental Analysis

Fundamental analysis focuses on the intrinsic value of a company. It involves studying a company's financial statements, industry conditions, economic factors, and other elements to determine whether the stock is undervalued or overvalued.

Key Components of Fundamental Analysis

Earnings Per Share (EPS):

EPS is one of the most important indicators of a company's profitability. It is calculated as:

$$EPS = \frac{Net\ Income}{Number\ of\ Shares\ Outstanding}$$

$$EPS = \frac{Number\ of\ Shares\ Outstanding}{Net\ Income}$$

Higher EPS indicates better profitability and is often seen as a good sign for investors.

Example:

If Tata Consultancy Services (TCS) has a net income of ₹10,000 crores and 100 crore shares outstanding, the EPS would be ₹100. This suggests that each share earned ₹100 for the company.

Price-to-Earnings Ratio (P/E Ratio):

The P/E ratio is a measure of how much investors are willing to pay for a company's earnings.

$$\text{P/E Ratio} = \frac{\text{Market Price Per Share}}{\text{EPS}}$$

$$\text{P/E Ratio} = \frac{\text{EPS}}{\text{Market Price Per Share}}$$

A high P/E ratio can indicate that the stock is overvalued or investors expect high future growth.

A low P/E ratio can suggest that the stock is undervalued or that the company is struggling.

Example:

If TCS has an EPS of ₹100, and its share price is ₹3,000, its P/E ratio would be 30 (₹3000 ÷ ₹100).

Compare this with a company like Coal India, which may have a P/E ratio of 10, indicating a more conservative valuation.

Return on Equity (ROE):

ROE measures how efficiently a company uses its equity to generate profits.

$$ROE = \frac{\text{Net Income}}{\text{Shareholder's Equity}}$$

$$ROE = \frac{\text{Shareholder's Equity}}{\text{Net Income}}$$

A higher ROE suggests the company is good at generating profits from shareholders' investments.

Example:

If Infosys generates ₹5,000 crore in net income and has ₹20,000 crore in equity, its ROE is 25% (₹5,000 crore ÷ ₹20,000 crore).

Debt-to-Equity Ratio (D/E Ratio):

This ratio shows how much debt a company has for each unit of equity.

D/E Ratio

=

Total Debt

Shareholder's Equity

D/E Ratio=

Shareholder's Equity

Total Debt

A high D/E ratio indicates that the company relies heavily on debt for funding, which can be risky.

Example:

If a company like Maruti Suzuki has a D/E ratio of 0.2, it suggests the company has a relatively low level of debt compared to its equity, which is generally seen as a safer investment.

Dividend Yield:

Dividend yield shows the annual dividends paid by a company as a percentage of its share price.

$$\text{Dividend Yield} = \frac{\text{Dividend per Share}}{\text{Share Price}} \times 100$$

Higher dividend yield can be attractive to income-seeking investors.

Example:

If HDFC Bank pays ₹50 per share in dividends and its stock price is ₹1,000, the dividend yield would be 5% (₹50 ÷ ₹1,000 × 100).

Qualitative Factors in Fundamental Analysis

In addition to financial ratios, investors should also consider qualitative factors such as:

Management quality: A strong management team often leads to better decision-making and performance.

Industry position: Companies with a dominant market share or competitive advantage tend to outperform others.

Economic conditions: Interest rates, inflation, and overall economic health can influence stock performance.

2. Technical Analysis

Technical analysis, on the other hand, focuses on studying price movements, volume, and historical trends to predict future stock price movements. It is mainly used for short-term trading.

Key Components of Technical Analysis

Price Charts:

Price charts visually represent a stock's price movements over time. The most common types are:

Line Charts

Bar Charts

Candlestick Charts (the most popular among traders)

Example:

A bullish candlestick pattern indicates that the stock price is likely to increase, while a bearish candlestick pattern suggests a potential decline.

Support and Resistance Levels:

Support: The price level at which a stock tends to find buying interest and thus prevents the price from falling further.

Resistance: The price level at which selling interest is strong enough to prevent the stock from rising further.

Example:

If a stock repeatedly rises to ₹500 but then falls back down, ₹500 is a resistance level. If it falls to ₹400 and then rises again, ₹400 is a support level.

Moving Averages (MA):

Moving averages smooth out price fluctuations over a specific period to identify trends.

Simple Moving Average (SMA): The average of prices over a set number of periods.

Exponential Moving Average (EMA): Gives more weight to recent prices, making it more sensitive to recent changes.

Example:

If the 50-day SMA crosses above the 200-day SMA, it is often seen as a bullish crossover, suggesting an upward trend.

Relative Strength Index (RSI):

The RSI measures the magnitude of recent price changes to evaluate overbought or oversold conditions. It ranges from 0 to 100, with values above 70 indicating overbought conditions and values below 30 indicating oversold conditions.

Example:

If a stock's RSI is at 80, it may be overbought and due for a correction. If it's at 20, it may be oversold and due for a rebound.

Volume Analysis:

Volume measures the number of shares traded. A price movement accompanied by high volume is considered more significant than one with low volume.

Example:

If a stock moves up by 5% on high volume, it's generally considered more sustainable than if the same movement occurs on low volume.

3. Combining Fundamental and Technical Analysis

While both approaches have their strengths, combining them provides a more comprehensive investment strategy.

Use Fundamental Analysis to identify undervalued stocks or strong companies for long-term investment.

Use Technical Analysis to time the entry and exit points for short-term trading.

Example:

Fundamental Approach: You find a solid company like HDFC Bank with excellent financials (high ROE, low debt-to-equity, and consistent earnings growth).

Technical Approach: On the chart, you notice a bullish candlestick pattern and a support level near ₹1,200, suggesting a good entry point.

Conclusion

Both fundamental and technical analysis are valuable tools for investors and traders. Fundamental analysis helps identify high-quality companies for long-term investments, while technical analysis aids in timing buy and sell decisions, especially for short-term traders. By understanding and applying both methods, you can make well-informed decisions that align with your investment goals and risk profile.

In the next chapter, we will explore the risks and rewards of stock market investing and how to manage them effectively.

Chapter 8: Risks and Rewards in Stock Market Investing

Investing in the stock market offers the potential for high returns, but it also comes with significant risks. Understanding the risks and rewards of stock market investing is crucial for making informed decisions and managing your investments effectively. In this chapter, we will explore the various types of risks and rewards associated with stock market investing, and provide practical tips on how to balance them in your portfolio.

1. The Rewards of Stock Market Investing

The stock market has historically provided one of the highest returns among different asset classes, though it comes with volatility. Let's break down the main rewards of investing in the stock market:

1.1. Capital Appreciation

What it is: Capital appreciation refers to the increase in the value of your investment over time.

How it works: When you buy stocks at a lower price and sell them at a higher price, the difference is your capital gain.

Example:

Suppose you bought 100 shares of Reliance Industries at ₹1,000 each. If the stock price rises to ₹2,000 after five years, you've made a ₹1,00,000 profit. The appreciation in value is the key reward of stock investing.

1.2. Dividends

What it is: Dividends are payments made by companies to their shareholders from their profits.

How it works: Not all companies pay dividends, but those that do offer a steady stream of income to shareholders, usually on a quarterly or annual basis.

Example:

If you own 500 shares of HDFC Bank, and the bank pays a dividend of ₹20 per share, you would receive ₹10,000 annually in dividend income. This income is a reward for holding the stock.

1.3. Liquidity

What it is: Liquidity refers to how easily an asset can be bought or sold without affecting its price significantly. Stocks are generally liquid because they are traded on stock exchanges.

How it works: If you need cash quickly, you can sell your stocks without much difficulty (depending on the stock's trading volume).

Example:

If you hold 100 shares of Tata Motors, you can quickly sell them on the stock market to convert them into cash. However, selling illiquid stocks can be difficult, as it might take time to find a buyer at the price you want.

1.4. Diversification Benefits

What it is: Diversification involves spreading your investments across different types of assets (stocks, bonds, real estate) to reduce risk.

How it works: By holding a diverse range of stocks, you reduce the risk of any single stock's poor performance affecting your overall portfolio.

Example:

A portfolio consisting of stocks from different sectors like Infosys (IT), Hindustan Unilever (Consumer Goods), and Bajaj Finance (Financials) can mitigate risks in case one sector underperforms.

1.5. Inflation Hedge

What it is: Stocks have the potential to outpace inflation over time. As companies grow and increase profits, stock prices often rise, keeping up with or exceeding the rate of inflation.

How it works: Stocks are generally a better hedge against inflation compared to bonds or cash, which can lose value in real terms over time due to rising prices.

Example:

Historically, the Indian stock market has provided annual returns of around 12-15%, which has outpaced inflation, allowing investors to preserve and grow their wealth.

2. The Risks of Stock Market Investing

While the stock market offers significant rewards, it also comes with inherent risks. Understanding these risks will help you make better decisions and mitigate potential losses.

2.1. Market Risk (Systematic Risk)

What it is: Market risk refers to the risk of losses due to factors that affect the entire market, such as economic downturns, interest rate changes, or geopolitical events.

How it works: This type of risk cannot be avoided through diversification because it affects all stocks.

Example:

During the 2008 global financial crisis, stock markets around the world saw significant declines, regardless of the company's fundamentals. A drop in stock prices due to broad market events is an example of market risk.

2.2. Stock-Specific Risk (Unsystematic Risk)

What it is: This is the risk associated with individual companies. Poor management, regulatory changes, competitive pressure, or other company-specific factors can affect the stock's price.

How it works: Diversification helps reduce unsystematic risk, as the poor performance of one stock might be offset by the good performance of others.

Example:

Satyam Computer Services (now Mahindra Susten) faced a major corporate governance scandal in 2009, which led to a sharp fall in its stock price, even though the broader market was stable at that time.

2.3. Liquidity Risk

What it is: Liquidity risk occurs when an investor is unable to sell a stock quickly without impacting its price. This typically affects stocks with low trading volumes.

How it works: If a stock is not actively traded, you might have to sell it at a lower price than you anticipated, or you might struggle to find a buyer at all.

Example:

Small-cap stocks like Suzlon Energy may be less liquid than large-cap stocks like HDFC Bank. If there's low demand for Suzlon shares, it may take time to sell them at a fair price.

2.4. Interest Rate Risk

What it is: Interest rate risk refers to the impact that changing interest rates have on the stock market. When interest rates rise, borrowing costs increase, potentially hurting corporate profits, which can lead to lower stock prices.

How it works: Stocks, especially those in interest-sensitive sectors like real estate or utilities, can see price declines when interest rates increase.

Example:

If the Reserve Bank of India (RBI) hikes interest rates, companies with high levels of debt, such as Realty Stocks (like DLF), may see a decline in stock prices as their borrowing costs rise.

2. 5. Inflation Risk

What it is: Inflation risk occurs when inflation outpaces the returns on your investments, eroding purchasing power.

How it works: If a stock's return is lower than the rate of inflation, your real return (after inflation) becomes negative, reducing your purchasing power.

Example:

If inflation is 7% and a stock only provides a 5% return, the investor's purchasing power decreases, as the returns don't keep pace with rising costs.

3. Balancing Risks and Rewards

Investors must find the right balance between risk and reward to achieve their financial goals. Here's how you can manage these risks effectively:

3.1. Diversification

What it is: Diversifying your investments across different asset classes (equities, bonds, real estate, etc.), sectors, and geographies helps reduce risk.

How it works: Diversification ensures that the poor performance of one investment doesn't significantly affect your overall portfolio.

Example:

A portfolio with a mix of blue-chip stocks like TCS (large-cap), mid-cap stocks like Lupin Pharmaceuticals, and bonds can lower risk.

3.2. Risk Tolerance Assessment

What it is: Risk tolerance is the degree of risk you are comfortable taking with your investments. It depends on your financial goals, time horizon, and personal preference.

How it works: Younger investors might take on more risk by investing in equities, while retirees may prefer safer options like bonds or fixed deposits.

Example:

A 25-year-old investor with a long-term horizon may afford to take more risk in stocks, whereas a 55-year-old investor nearing retirement may prefer bonds to preserve capital.

3.3. Regular Portfolio Review

What it is: Regularly reviewing and rebalancing your portfolio ensures that it remains aligned with your goals and risk tolerance.

How it works: If the stock market performs well, equities may take up a larger portion of your portfolio. You may need to sell some equities and buy bonds or other assets to maintain your desired asset allocation.

Example:

If your portfolio's equity allocation has risen to 80% due to a market rally, and your target allocation is 60%, you may sell some equities and reinvest the proceeds in bonds.

4. Conclusion

Stock market investing offers the potential for high returns, but it also involves substantial risks. To succeed, you must understand the rewards you can expect and the risks you are taking. The key to successful investing lies in balancing these risks with your rewards through strategies like diversification, understanding your risk tolerance, and regular portfolio reviews. By being aware of the risks and rewards, you can make more informed decisions that align with your financial goals.

The next chapter will cover the strategies for long-term success in the stock market, focusing on building a disciplined investment approach for sustainable wealth creation.

Chapter 9: Strategies for Long-Term Success in the Stock Market

Success in the stock market is not about making quick gains but about building wealth over time through consistent and disciplined investing. In this chapter, we'll explore proven strategies that can help you achieve long-term success, minimize risks, and maximize returns.

1. Setting Clear Financial Goals

The foundation of successful investing begins with clear financial goals.

1.1. Importance of Goal Setting

Goals help you define the purpose of your investments, whether it's wealth creation, buying a house, funding education, or retirement planning.

Goals determine your risk tolerance, time horizon, and investment choices.

1.2. Categorizing Goals

Short-term goals: Achieving them within 1–3 years, such as saving for a vacation.

Medium-term goals: Achieving them in 3–7 years, such as purchasing a car.

Long-term goals: Achieving them over 7+ years, such as retirement planning.

Example:

Short-term: Save ₹5,00,000 for a wedding in 2 years.

Long-term: Build a corpus of ₹2 crore for retirement in 25 years.

2. Start Early and Stay Invested

One of the most powerful strategies for long-term success is starting early.

2.1. Power of Compounding

Compounding allows your investments to generate earnings, and those earnings are reinvested to generate additional earnings.

The earlier you start, the longer compounding can work for you.

Example:

Investor A starts investing ₹10,000 per month at the age of 25 and stops at 35 (invests for 10 years).

Investor B starts investing ₹10,000 per month at the age of 35 and continues until 60 (invests for 25 years).

Assuming a 12% annual return, Investor A ends up with ₹1.54 crore, while Investor B ends up with ₹1.28 crore, even though B invested for a longer duration.

3. Diversification

Diversification reduces risk by spreading investments across various asset classes, sectors, and geographies.

3.1. Asset Classes

Equities: Higher risk, higher return potential.

Bonds: Lower risk, steady income.

Real Estate: Inflation hedge and potential capital appreciation.

Gold: Safe-haven asset during uncertainty.

3.2. Sector Diversification

Investing in different sectors ensures that poor performance in one sector doesn't significantly impact your portfolio.

Example:

A portfolio that includes IT stocks (Infosys), Banking (HDFC Bank), FMCG (Hindustan Unilever), and Pharma (Sun Pharma) is more resilient than one concentrated in a single sector.

4. Adopt a Systematic Investment Plan (SIP)

SIP is a disciplined way of investing small amounts regularly in mutual funds or stocks.

4.1. Benefits of SIP

Rupee cost averaging: You buy more units when prices are low and fewer units when prices are high, reducing the overall cost per unit.

Discipline: SIPs eliminate the need to time the market and instill a habit of regular investing.

Example:

If you invest ₹5,000 monthly in an equity mutual fund for 20 years at a 12% annual return, your corpus will grow to approximately ₹50 lakh.

5. Focus on Quality Stocks

Investing in high-quality companies with strong fundamentals is key to long-term success.

5.1. Characteristics of Quality Stocks

Consistent earnings growth.

Low debt-to-equity ratio.

High return on equity (ROE).

Competitive advantages (e.g., brand, technology).

Example:

Companies like Reliance Industries, TCS, and HDFC Bank have a history of strong performance and sound fundamentals, making them suitable for long-term investments.

6. Reinvest Dividends

Dividends can significantly boost your returns over time if reinvested.

6.1. Impact of Dividend Reinvestment

When dividends are reinvested, they generate additional returns, creating a compounding effect.

Example:

If you invest ₹1,00,000 in a stock with an annual dividend yield of 4% and reinvest the dividends at a 10% annual return, your investment grows faster than if you took the dividends as cash.

7. Stay Informed but Avoid Overtrading

7.1. Stay Updated

Follow economic news, company updates, and market trends to make informed decisions.

Regularly review your portfolio and align it with changing market conditions.

7.2. Avoid Overtrading

Overtrading increases transaction costs and taxes, eating into your returns.

Emotional trading, driven by fear or greed, often leads to poor decisions.

Example:

During market corrections, avoid panic-selling quality stocks. Historical data shows that markets recover over time, rewarding patient investors.

8. Manage Risk Through Asset Allocation

Asset allocation is the process of dividing your investments among different asset classes based on your risk tolerance and goals.

8.1. Age-Based Asset Allocation

A common rule of thumb is to subtract your age from 100 to determine the percentage of your portfolio to allocate to equities.

Example:

At age 30: 70% equities, 30% bonds.

At age 60: 40% equities, 60% bonds.

9. Learn from Mistakes and Stay Disciplined

9.1. Common Mistakes to Avoid

Timing the market: Trying to predict short-term market movements often leads to losses.

Lack of diversification: Concentrating investments in one stock or sector increases risk.

Ignoring fees and taxes: High transaction fees and taxes can erode returns.

9.2. Stick to Your Plan

Avoid making impulsive decisions based on market volatility.

Stay committed to your investment strategy, even during downturns.

10. Have a Long-Term Perspective

10.1. Ignore Short-Term Noise

Stock prices fluctuate daily, but long-term investors focus on the underlying value of their investments.

Historical data shows that markets reward patience and discipline over time.

10.2. Historical Example: Sensex Growth

The BSE Sensex, which was at 100 points in 1979, crossed 60,000 points in 2021. Despite multiple market crashes and corrections, long-term investors who stayed invested reaped substantial rewards.

Conclusion

Long-term success in the stock market requires a combination of knowledge, discipline, and patience. By setting clear goals, starting early, diversifying, and staying committed to a sound strategy, you can navigate market ups and downs and achieve your financial objectives. Remember, investing is a marathon, not a sprint. Stay focused on your goals, and let time and compounding work their magic.

In the next chapter, we will explore building a balanced portfolio, offering practical guidance on constructing and maintaining a portfolio that aligns with your goals and risk tolerance.

Chapter 10: Building and Managing a Balanced Portfolio

A well-balanced portfolio is the cornerstone of successful investing. It not only helps achieve your financial goals but also mitigates risks by spreading investments across various asset classes. In this chapter, we will dive into the concept of portfolio balancing, the factors to consider, and strategies to build and manage a portfolio effectively.

1. What is a Balanced Portfolio?

A balanced portfolio is a mix of investments designed to achieve an optimal balance between risk and reward. The goal is to diversify investments across different asset classes, sectors, and geographies to minimize the impact of underperforming assets on the overall portfolio.

2. The Importance of a Balanced Portfolio

2.1. Risk Management

Diversification ensures that losses in one asset class are offset by gains in another.

It reduces volatility, providing more stable returns over time.

2.2. Meeting Financial Goals

A balanced portfolio aligns with your financial objectives and risk tolerance, helping you stay on track to meet your goals.

2.3. Adapting to Market Conditions

Different assets perform well under different market conditions. A balanced portfolio can capitalize on this.

Example: In 2020, while equity markets were volatile due to COVID-19, gold provided excellent returns, acting as a hedge in a balanced portfolio.

3. Components of a Balanced Portfolio

3.1. Asset Classes

A balanced portfolio typically includes a mix of:

Equities

Growth potential but high risk.

Suitable for long-term goals.

Bonds

Provides stability and regular income.

Acts as a buffer during market downturns.

Real Estate

Offers capital appreciation and an inflation hedge.

Less liquid compared to other assets.

Gold

A safe-haven asset during uncertainty.

Acts as a hedge against inflation.

Cash and Cash Equivalents

Provides liquidity for emergencies or opportunities.

Includes fixed deposits, treasury bills, etc.

4. Steps to Build a Balanced Portfolio

4.1. Define Your Financial Goals

Short-term goals: Require liquidity and low-risk investments like bonds or cash equivalents.

Long-term goals: Can accommodate higher-risk, high-reward assets like equities.

Example: If your goal is to save ₹10 lakh for a child's education in 3 years, focus on safe assets. For retirement in 20 years, prioritize equities.

4.2. Assess Your Risk Tolerance

Conservative Investor: Prefers stability; lower allocation to equities.

Aggressive Investor: Willing to take risks for higher returns; higher allocation to equities.

4.3. Determine Your Asset Allocation

Asset allocation is the process of deciding how much of your portfolio to invest in each asset class. It depends on your age, risk tolerance, and financial goals.

Rule of Thumb:

Subtract your age from 100 to determine your equity allocation. The remainder goes into safer assets like bonds.

Example: At age 30, allocate 70% to equities and 30% to bonds and other safer investments.

4.4. Diversify Within Asset Classes

Equities: Spread across large-cap, mid-cap, and small-cap stocks, and across sectors like IT, healthcare, and banking.

Bonds: Include government securities, corporate bonds, and fixed deposits.

Real Estate: Invest in both residential and commercial properties or Real Estate Investment Trusts (REITs).

Gold: Invest in physical gold, gold ETFs, or sovereign gold bonds.

5. Rebalancing Your Portfolio

Over time, market movements can skew your portfolio's allocation. Regular rebalancing helps maintain the desired risk level.

5.1. How to Rebalance

Sell overperforming assets and invest in underperforming ones to restore your original allocation.

Review your portfolio at least annually or when there are significant market changes.

Example: If equities outperform and now make up 80% of your portfolio (from the intended 70%), sell a portion of equities and reinvest in bonds or other assets.

6. Common Portfolio Strategies

6.1. Conservative Portfolio

High allocation to bonds and cash equivalents (70–80%).

Low allocation to equities (20–30%).

Suitable for risk-averse investors or those nearing retirement.

6.2. Balanced Portfolio

Equal allocation to equities and bonds (50–50%).

Provides moderate risk and return.

Suitable for investors with a medium risk tolerance.

6.3. Aggressive Portfolio

High allocation to equities (70–80%).

Low allocation to bonds and cash equivalents (20–30%).

Suitable for younger investors with a long investment horizon.

7. Real-Life Example of a Balanced Portfolio

Case Study: Raj's Investment Plan

Age: 35

Goal: Save ₹3 crore for retirement in 25 years.

Initial Portfolio:

Equities: 60% (₹6,00,000 in mutual funds and direct stocks).

Bonds: 30% (₹3,00,000 in government bonds and fixed deposits).

Gold: 5% (₹50,000 in gold ETFs).

Cash: 5% (₹50,000 in a savings account).

Annual Rebalancing:

After a year, equities grow to ₹7,00,000, bonds remain at ₹3,00,000, gold increases to ₹55,000, and cash stays at ₹50,000. Raj rebalances by selling ₹1,00,000 worth of equities and reinvesting in bonds to restore the 60–30–5–5 allocation.

8. Challenges in Managing a Balanced Portfolio

8.1. Emotional Decision-Making

Fear and greed can lead to impulsive decisions.

Avoid panic-selling during market downturns or overinvesting during rallies.

8.2. Ignoring Costs

High transaction fees, taxes, and fund management charges can erode returns.

8.3. Lack of Regular Monitoring

A neglected portfolio may become too risky or too conservative over time.

9. Tools for Portfolio Management

9.1. Portfolio Tracking Apps

Apps like Zerodha Console, ET Money, and Groww help track investments.

9.2. Financial Advisors

Seek professional advice to build and manage a portfolio tailored to your needs.

9.3. Online Platforms

Platforms like Morningstar and Moneycontrol offer tools for portfolio analysis and rebalancing.

10. Conclusion

Building and managing a balanced portfolio is a dynamic process that requires planning, discipline, and regular review. By understanding your financial goals, risk tolerance, and time horizon, and following a structured approach, you can create a portfolio that provides stability and growth. The key to success is staying disciplined, avoiding emotional decisions, and regularly rebalancing your investments.

In the next chapter, we will delve into Analyzing Market Trends and Economic Indicators, helping you make informed investment decisions based on market movements and macroeconomic factors.

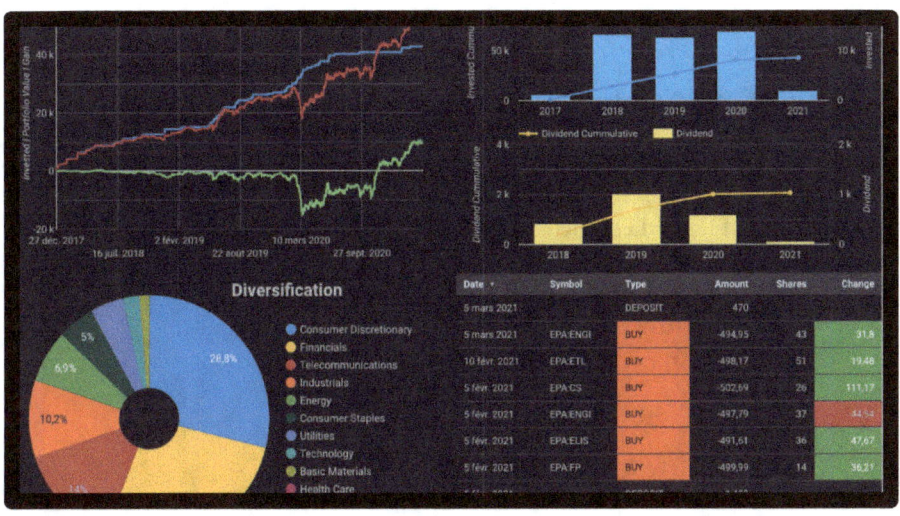

Chapter 11: Analyzing Market Trends and Economic Indicators

Understanding market trends and economic indicators is crucial for making informed investment decisions. This chapter explains how to interpret various signals from the market and the economy to enhance your ability to evaluate investments effectively.

1. What are Market Trends?

Market trends refer to the general direction in which the market or a particular asset class is moving over time. Identifying trends can help investors decide when to enter or exit the market.

1.1. Types of Market Trends

Uptrend (Bullish Market):

Characterized by rising stock prices.

Indicates investor confidence and strong economic conditions.

Downtrend (Bearish Market):

Characterized by falling stock prices.

Reflects pessimism or economic challenges.

Sideways Trend:

Market moves within a narrow range.

Often signals uncertainty or a lack of clear direction.

2. Tools for Analyzing Market Trends

2.1. Technical Analysis

Technical analysis involves studying price charts, patterns, and trading volumes to predict future movements.

Key Tools:

Moving Averages: Helps smooth price data to identify trends.

Relative Strength Index (RSI): Indicates whether a stock is overbought or oversold.

Support and Resistance Levels: Highlight price points where stocks tend to reverse direction.

Example: If a stock consistently trades above its 200-day moving average, it is considered to be in an uptrend.

2.2. Fundamental Analysis

Fundamental analysis focuses on evaluating a company's intrinsic value by analyzing its financial statements, industry position, and macroeconomic factors.

Key Metrics:

Price-to-Earnings (P/E) ratio.

Earnings per Share (EPS).

Debt-to-Equity Ratio.

Example: A low P/E ratio compared to industry peers might indicate that a stock is undervalued.

3. Understanding Economic Indicators

Economic indicators provide insights into the overall health of the economy. They are broadly categorized into leading, lagging, and coincident indicators.

3.1. Leading Indicators

These predict future economic trends and are useful for proactive decision-making.

Examples:

Stock market performance.

Manufacturing Purchasing Managers' Index (PMI).

Consumer confidence index.

Interpretation: A rising PMI often indicates economic expansion, encouraging investors to take bullish positions.

3.2. Lagging Indicators

These confirm past economic performance and help validate trends.

Examples:

Gross Domestic Product (GDP) growth rate.

Unemployment rate.

Corporate profits.

Interpretation: An increasing GDP growth rate confirms that the economy is performing well.

3.3. Coincident Indicators

These reflect current economic conditions.

Examples:

Retail sales data.

Industrial production.

Job creation numbers.

Interpretation: Steady retail sales suggest robust consumer spending, a positive signal for the economy.

4. Interpreting Market Sentiment

Market sentiment reflects the overall attitude of investors toward a particular market or asset.

4.1. Fear and Greed Index

Measures emotions driving the market.

High levels of fear may indicate undervalued stocks, while excessive greed could signal overvaluation.

4.2. Volatility Index (VIX)

Known as the "fear gauge."

A rising VIX indicates market uncertainty and potential volatility.

Example: During the COVID-19 pandemic, the VIX spiked significantly, reflecting high levels of fear and uncertainty.

5. Analyzing Global Economic Indicators

Global events and economic data significantly impact the Indian stock market, especially in an interconnected world.

5.1. US Federal Reserve Policy

Interest rate hikes or cuts by the US Federal Reserve affect global liquidity and market sentiment.

5.2. Crude Oil Prices

Rising crude prices increase import costs for India, impacting inflation and corporate profitability.

5.3. Currency Exchange Rates

A weakening rupee can hurt companies relying on imports but benefit exporters.

6. Impact of Domestic Economic Policies

Government policies, such as fiscal measures, interest rates, and taxation, play a significant role in shaping market trends.

6.1. Fiscal Policy

Increased government spending on infrastructure boosts sectors like construction and cement.

6.2. Monetary Policy

A reduction in interest rates by the Reserve Bank of India (RBI) encourages borrowing, boosting economic activity.

Example: The RBI's rate cuts in 2020 to combat the pandemic-induced slowdown led to a surge in real estate and automobile sales.

7. Sector-Specific Analysis

Analyzing sector-specific trends helps identify opportunities within industries.

7.1. IT Sector

Strong global demand for technology services can drive growth.

Keep an eye on the NASDAQ performance, as it influences Indian IT companies.

7.2. Banking Sector

A rising interest rate environment can benefit banks due to higher net interest margins.

7.3. Pharma Sector

Regulatory approvals and export trends are critical factors to monitor.

8. Practical Application: Combining Indicators

Investors often use a mix of tools and indicators to develop a comprehensive view of the market.

Example:

If the GDP growth rate is rising (lagging indicator) and the PMI is above 50 (leading indicator), the economic outlook is positive.

Combine this with technical analysis showing stocks above their 50-day moving averages, signaling an uptrend.

9. Challenges in Analyzing Market Trends

9.1. Information Overload

Too much data can lead to confusion and analysis paralysis.

9.2. Emotional Bias

Overreacting to short-term market movements can disrupt long-term strategies.

9.3. Unpredictable Events

Black swan events, such as pandemics or geopolitical tensions, can disrupt even well-analyzed predictions.

10. Conclusion

Analyzing market trends and economic indicators is both an art and a science. By combining technical tools, fundamental analysis, and macroeconomic data, investors can make informed decisions and align their strategies with market conditions. However, no analysis guarantees success, so it's essential to remain disciplined, diversify, and focus on long-term goals.

In the next chapter, we will explore Behavioral Finance, diving into how psychological factors influence investment decisions and strategies to overcome common biases.

Chapter 12: Behavioral Finance – Psychology of Investing

Behavioral finance explores the psychological factors and biases that influence investors' decisions. Understanding these concepts can help investors avoid common pitfalls and make rational, informed decisions.

1. What is Behavioral Finance?

Behavioral finance combines psychology and economics to explain why people make irrational financial decisions. It focuses on how emotions, cognitive errors, and biases impact investment behavior.

Example: During a market crash, many investors panic and sell their stocks, locking in losses, even though staying invested may yield better long-term results.

2. Common Behavioral Biases

2.1. Herd Mentality

Investors follow the crowd without independent analysis.

Leads to bubbles (e.g., dot-com bubble) or mass sell-offs.

Example: The cryptocurrency boom of 2017 saw many investing purely because "everyone else was doing it," without understanding the technology.

How to Overcome:

Research independently.

Avoid decisions based solely on peer pressure.

2.2. Overconfidence Bias

Investors overestimate their ability to predict market movements.

Leads to excessive risk-taking and overtrading.

Example: An investor who earns high returns during a bull market might attribute it to skill rather than favorable conditions.

How to Overcome:

Regularly review and question your investment decisions.

Diversify to mitigate risks.

2.3. Loss Aversion

Fear of losses is stronger than the pleasure of gains.

Leads to holding onto losing investments too long or selling winners prematurely.

Example: An investor holds onto a poorly performing stock hoping it will recover, even when better opportunities exist.

How to Overcome:

Set clear exit strategies.

Focus on portfolio performance rather than individual investments.

2.4. Anchoring Bias

Relying too heavily on an initial piece of information.

Leads to sticking to outdated valuations or expectations.

Example: An investor who bought a stock at ₹500 may hesitate to sell at ₹450, even if the fundamentals have worsened.

How to Overcome:

Base decisions on current data, not historical prices.

2.5. Confirmation Bias

Seeking information that supports pre-existing beliefs while ignoring contrary evidence.

Example: An investor bullish on a stock only reads positive news about the company and ignores warnings from analysts.

How to Overcome:

Actively seek opposing viewpoints.

Regularly reassess your assumptions.

3. Emotional Traps in Investing

3.1. Fear and Greed

Fear leads to panic selling; greed results in overexposure to risky assets.

Example: Investors rushed into tech stocks during the late 1990s driven by greed, only to face massive losses when the bubble burst.

How to Overcome:

Stick to a predefined strategy.

Avoid emotional reactions to market swings.

3.2. Impatience

Expecting quick gains leads to abandoning long-term strategies.

Example: Selling a mutual fund after one year of low returns, even though it has a strong 10-year performance track record.

How to Overcome:

Align investments with your time horizon.

Track performance over appropriate periods.

4. Behavioral Finance and Market Phenomena

4.1. Market Bubbles

Driven by irrational exuberance and herd behavior.

Prices rise far above intrinsic values.

Example: The dot-com bubble of the late 1990s saw internet companies trading at astronomical valuations without profits.

4.2. Market Crashes

Caused by panic selling, often exacerbated by loss aversion and fear.

Investors abandon long-term plans during downturns.

Example: The 2008 financial crisis saw widespread sell-offs, even in fundamentally sound companies.

5. Strategies to Overcome Behavioral Biases

5.1. Establish a Clear Investment Plan

Define your goals, risk tolerance, and time horizon.

Stick to the plan regardless of market conditions.

5.2. Automate Investments

Use systematic investment plans (SIPs) to remove emotional decision-making.

Helps average out costs over time.

5.3. Regular Portfolio Reviews

Rebalance your portfolio periodically to align with your goals.

Prevents overexposure to specific assets.

5.4. Educate Yourself

Learn about behavioral biases to recognize and counteract them.

Stay updated on market trends and economic conditions.

5.5. Seek Professional Guidance

Financial advisors can provide objective advice and counter emotional reactions.

6. Real-Life Case Studies

Case Study 1: The Tulip Mania (1630s)

Tulip bulbs in the Netherlands were traded at exorbitant prices due to herd behavior.

When prices crashed, many were left with worthless investments.

Case Study 2: Bitcoin Bubble (2017)

Bitcoin reached nearly $20,000 due to speculative buying.

Prices plummeted to under $4,000 within a year, showcasing the dangers of overconfidence and herd mentality.

7. Benefits of Behavioral Finance Awareness

Improved Decision-Making: Recognizing biases leads to better investment choices.

Reduced Emotional Impact: Helps maintain discipline during volatile markets.

Enhanced Long-Term Returns: Staying focused on fundamentals rather than noise prevents costly mistakes.

8. Conclusion

Behavioral finance highlights the importance of understanding the human side of investing. By recognizing and addressing your biases, you can make more rational decisions and avoid common pitfalls. Remember, successful investing requires discipline, patience, and continuous learning.

Chapter 13: Building a Long-Term Investment Strategy

A long-term investment strategy is essential for achieving financial goals, creating wealth, and maintaining financial stability. This chapter focuses on the principles, processes, and tools required to develop and sustain a successful long-term investment plan.

1. Importance of a Long-Term Investment Strategy

1.1. Wealth Accumulation

Compounding allows investments to grow exponentially over time.

Long-term strategies minimize the impact of short-term market volatility.

Example: Investing ₹10,000 per month in a mutual fund with an annual return of 12% will grow to ₹1.1 crore in 20 years.

1.2. Goal-Oriented Investing

Helps achieve major life goals, such as purchasing a home, funding education, or retirement planning.

Aligns investments with specific timelines.

1.3. Tax Efficiency

Long-term investments often attract lower taxes, enhancing net returns.

2. Defining Financial Goals

Financial goals are the foundation of any investment strategy. Categorize them as follows:

Short-Term Goals: Achievable within 1-3 years (e.g., vacation, emergency fund).

Medium-Term Goals: Achievable within 3-7 years (e.g., buying a car, higher education).

Long-Term Goals: Achievable in 7+ years (e.g., retirement, children's marriage).

Example of Goal Setting: Rahul plans to retire in 20 years with a corpus of ₹2 crore. He calculates that investing ₹25,000 per month in a portfolio yielding 10% annually will help him reach his target.

3. Steps to Build a Long-Term Investment Strategy

3.1. Assess Your Financial Situation

Calculate your income, expenses, and savings.

Understand your risk tolerance and time horizon.

3.2. Diversify Investments

Spread investments across asset classes (equity, debt, gold, real estate) to reduce risk.

3.3. Choose Suitable Investment Vehicles

For long-term goals:

Equities and Mutual Funds: High growth potential.

PPF and EPF: Stable returns with tax benefits.

NPS: Ideal for retirement planning.

3.4. Automate Investments

Systematic Investment Plans (SIPs) ensure disciplined investing.

Automation helps in maintaining consistency.

3.5. Monitor and Rebalance

Review portfolio performance periodically.

Reallocate funds to maintain the desired asset mix.

4. Key Principles of Long-Term Investing

4.1. Patience

Avoid reacting to short-term market fluctuations.

Focus on long-term potential rather than immediate returns.

4.2. Discipline

Stick to your investment plan, even during volatile market phases.

Consistency ensures compounding works in your favor.

4.3. Risk Management

Avoid overexposure to risky assets.

Use diversified portfolios to cushion against market downturns.

4.4. Regular Contributions

Small, consistent investments grow into substantial wealth over time.

5. Asset Allocation and Portfolio Management

5.1. Asset Allocation

Distribute investments across asset classes based on risk tolerance and goals.

Example: For a 30-year-old with moderate risk tolerance:

- 60% in equities.
- 30% in debt instruments.
- 10% in gold or alternative investments.

5.2. Portfolio Management

Dynamic management to adapt to changing goals and market conditions.

Use a core-satellite approach:

- Core Portfolio: Stable, long-term investments.
- Satellite Portfolio: Tactical investments for short-term opportunities.

6. Common Mistakes in Long-Term Investing

6.1. Lack of Planning

Investing without clear goals or strategy can lead to suboptimal results.

6.2. Emotional Decision-Making

Panic selling during market downturns or over-investing in bull markets harms returns.

6.3. Ignoring Inflation

Failing to consider inflation erodes the real value of savings over time.

6.4. Overlooking Rebalancing

Skipping periodic portfolio reviews can lead to imbalances and increased risk.

7. Tools for Long-Term Investing

7.1. Financial Calculators

Use SIP calculators, retirement planners, and goal-based tools to estimate requirements.

7.2. Mobile Apps and Platforms

Apps like Zerodha, Groww, and CAMS simplify tracking and managing investments.

7.3. Robo-Advisors

Automated platforms provide tailored investment recommendations.

8. Real-Life Case Studies

Case Study 1: The Power of SIPs

Neha started a SIP of ₹5,000 per month at age 25, achieving an annual return of 12%. By 45, her investment grew to ₹50 lakh.

Case Study 2: Long-Term Equity Growth

Aman invested ₹1 lakh in a blue-chip stock in 2000. Over 20 years, the stock delivered a CAGR of 15%, growing to over ₹16 lakh.

9. Conclusion

Building a long-term investment strategy requires careful planning, discipline, and patience. By setting clear goals, diversifying, and staying consistent, you can navigate market fluctuations and achieve financial independence. Remember, the earlier you start, the greater the power of compounding to grow your wealth.

In the next chapter, we will discuss The Role of Technology in Modern Investing, exploring how advancements have revolutionized investment strategies and accessibility.

Chapter 14: The Role of Technology in Modern Investing

Technology has significantly transformed the investment landscape, making it more accessible, efficient, and inclusive. This chapter delves into the various ways technology has reshaped modern investing, offering tools, platforms, and strategies that empower investors.

1. The Evolution of Investing Through Technology

Investing has evolved from traditional methods like physical share certificates and manual trading to seamless, digital platforms.

1.1. Before Technology

Investors relied on brokers for transactions.

Limited access to information and data.

Manual processes with higher fees and delays.

1.2. After Technological Advancements

Online platforms and apps enable self-directed investing.

Real-time market data and analysis are widely available.

Automation and AI simplify decision-making and portfolio management.

2. Key Technological Innovations in Investing

2.1. Online Trading Platforms

Allow investors to buy and sell securities from anywhere.

Examples: Zerodha, Upstox, Angel Broking.

2.2. Mobile Apps

Provide easy access to portfolios, research, and market updates.

Features include alerts, SIP management, and goal tracking.

Example: Apps like Groww and Paytm Money let users invest in mutual funds, stocks, and even gold in a few clicks.

2.3. Robo-Advisors

Automated platforms that provide personalized investment advice.

Use algorithms to create and manage portfolios based on goals and risk tolerance.

Example: Platforms like Scripbox and Kuvera offer low-cost, AI-driven portfolio management.

2.4. Artificial Intelligence (AI) and Machine Learning (ML)

Analyze large datasets to predict market trends and identify opportunities.

AI-powered tools assist in stock screening, portfolio optimization, and risk assessment.

2.5. Blockchain and Cryptocurrency

Blockchain ensures transparency and security in financial transactions.

Cryptocurrencies like Bitcoin and Ethereum have emerged as alternative investment options.

2.6. Algorithmic Trading

Uses predefined rules and algorithms to execute trades automatically.

Enables high-frequency trading with minimal human intervention.

3. Benefits of Technology in Investing

3.1. Accessibility

Low entry barriers enable even small investors to participate.

Fractional shares and SIPs make investing affordable.

3.2. Cost Efficiency

Reduced brokerage fees and management costs.

Free tools and apps offer professional-grade analysis.

3.3. Real-Time Insights

Access to live market data and news ensures informed decisions.

Predictive analytics highlight opportunities.

3.4. Automation

SIPs, recurring deposits, and automated rebalancing simplify wealth creation.

Reduces emotional decision-making.

4. Challenges of Technology in Investing

4.1. Over-Reliance on Tools

Blindly following algorithms can lead to suboptimal outcomes.

4.2. Security Concerns

Risk of data breaches and cyber fraud.

Importance of choosing secure platforms with encryption.

4.3. Information Overload

Excessive data can overwhelm and confuse investors.

4.4. Misuse of Technology

High-frequency trading can distort markets.

Speculative trading apps may encourage gambling behavior.

5. How to Leverage Technology for Smart Investing

5.1. Choose Reliable Platforms

Opt for SEBI-registered brokers and verified apps.

Check reviews and security features.

5.2. Use Data Analytics Tools

Explore tools like TradingView and MarketSmith for in-depth analysis.

5.3. Combine AI with Human Judgment

Use AI-driven insights but verify with personal research and logic.

5.4. Stay Updated

Follow blogs, podcasts, and webinars to keep up with technological trends.

6. Real-Life Case Studies

Case Study 1: SIP Automation for Goal Achievement

Ravi used an app to automate his SIPs in equity mutual funds. Over 10 years, his disciplined approach helped him save ₹15 lakh for his child's education.

Case Study 2: Robo-Advisors Simplify Retirement Planning

Seema relied on a robo-advisory platform to create a diversified retirement portfolio. The automated rebalancing ensured her portfolio remained aligned with her goals.

7. The Future of Technology in Investing

7.1. AI-Driven Financial Advisors

Personalized investment recommendations based on real-time data.

7.2. Tokenization of Assets

Fractional ownership of high-value assets like real estate and art.

7.3. Decentralized Finance (DeFi)

Peer-to-peer lending and borrowing without traditional intermediaries.

7.4. Enhanced Virtual Reality (VR) Tools

Immersive simulations for understanding complex financial concepts.

8. Conclusion

Technology has democratized investing, making it accessible and efficient for all. By leveraging tools like AI, robo-advisors, and blockchain, investors can make smarter decisions and achieve financial independence.

However, staying informed and vigilant about potential risks is crucial.

In the final chapter, we will discuss Common Mistakes to Avoid in Investing, equipping you with the knowledge to sidestep errors and maximize your success.

Chapter 15: Common Mistakes to Avoid in Investing

Investing is a journey that requires knowledge, discipline, and the ability to learn from mistakes. However, many investors fall into common traps that hinder their progress and reduce returns. In this chapter, we will explore these pitfalls and provide actionable tips to avoid them.

1. Lack of Clear Financial Goals

Investing without clear objectives often leads to scattered and ineffective efforts. Without goals, it's hard to measure success or choose the right investments.

How to Avoid:

Set SMART goals (Specific, Measurable, Achievable, Relevant, Time-bound).

Example: Instead of saying, "I want to save for retirement," set a goal like, "I will save ₹2 crore for retirement in 20 years by investing ₹20,000 per month."

2. Insufficient Research

Many investors rely on hearsay, hot tips, or speculative advice without conducting thorough research.

How to Avoid:

Analyze the company's fundamentals before buying shares.

Use trusted financial tools and platforms for insights.

Example: Instead of investing in a trending stock because a friend recommended it, review its financial statements, growth prospects, and industry trends.

3. Emotional Decision-Making

Emotions like fear and greed can lead to impulsive decisions, such as panic selling during market downturns or overbuying in a bull run.

How to Avoid:

Stick to a pre-defined investment plan.

Avoid checking portfolio performance excessively to reduce anxiety.

Example: During a market crash, instead of selling in panic, evaluate if the fundamentals of your investments remain strong.

4. Overlooking Diversification

Putting all your money in one asset class or stock increases risk significantly.

How to Avoid:

Diversify across asset classes (equity, debt, gold, etc.).

Allocate investments based on risk tolerance and goals.

Example: A balanced portfolio might include 50% in equities, 30% in debt, and 20% in gold or real estate.

5. Ignoring Inflation

Investing in instruments with low returns may not beat inflation, eroding the real value of your money.

How to Avoid:

Opt for growth-oriented investments like equities for long-term goals.

Example: Instead of keeping all your money in a savings account earning 4% interest, invest in a mutual fund with a potential return of 10-12%.

6. Timing the Market

Trying to predict market highs and lows often leads to missed opportunities and losses.

How to Avoid:

Focus on time in the market, not timing the market.

Use Systematic Investment Plans (SIPs) to average out purchase costs.

Example: Instead of waiting for the "perfect" time to invest, start with a SIP in a mutual fund and benefit from rupee cost averaging.

7. Neglecting Emergency Funds

Investing without an emergency fund may force you to liquidate investments prematurely during financial crises.

How to Avoid:

Maintain an emergency fund covering 6-12 months of expenses.

Example: Before investing in equities, ensure you have ₹3-6 lakh in a liquid savings account or short-term debt fund if your monthly expenses are ₹50,000.

8. Ignoring Tax Implications

Overlooking taxation can reduce net returns significantly.

How to Avoid:

Understand tax rules for various instruments (e.g., LTCG, STCG, dividend tax).

Invest in tax-saving instruments like ELSS, PPF, and NPS where applicable.

Example: Selling equity shares after one year qualifies for LTCG tax, which is lower than STCG for short-term holdings.

9. Chasing High Returns

Investors often prioritize returns without assessing the associated risks.

How to Avoid:

Evaluate the risk-return trade-off for every investment.

Avoid schemes promising unusually high returns; they could be scams.

Example: Instead of chasing a scheme claiming a 20% monthly return, consider a diversified equity mutual fund offering sustainable annual growth of 10-12%.

10. Lack of Regular Portfolio Review (continued)

Failing to review and rebalance portfolios can lead to misaligned investments and risk exposure. Over time, market movements may shift the allocation of your assets, increasing your risk beyond acceptable levels.

How to Avoid:

Conduct portfolio reviews at least annually or after major life events.

Rebalance to maintain your desired asset allocation.

Example: If your equity allocation grows from 50% to 70% due to a bull market, sell some equity investments and reinvest in debt to restore balance.

11. Overtrading

Frequent buying and selling of securities lead to high transaction costs and potential tax liabilities, which erode returns.

How to Avoid:

Adopt a long-term perspective.

Avoid making impulsive trades based on daily market news.

Example: Instead of frequently buying and selling stocks, hold quality stocks for the long term to benefit from compounding and capital appreciation.

12. Investing Without Understanding

Investing in complex instruments or schemes without sufficient knowledge can lead to losses.

How to Avoid:

Educate yourself about investment options.

Consult with a financial advisor for guidance.

Example: Before investing in derivatives or futures, understand how they work and the risks involved.

13. Failing to Account for Risk Tolerance

Investing in high-risk assets without assessing your ability to bear losses can lead to financial stress.

How to Avoid:

Evaluate your risk tolerance based on age, income, and financial goals.

Choose investments that align with your risk profile.

Example: A young investor may allocate more to equities, while a retiree might prefer debt and fixed-income instruments.

14. Ignoring Professional Advice

While DIY investing is appealing, ignoring expert advice may result in missed opportunities or poor decisions.

How to Avoid:

Seek professional advice when required, especially for complex financial planning.

Use hybrid approaches—combine self-directed investing with expert input.

Example: Consult a financial planner for tax optimization and estate planning while managing a basic equity portfolio independently.

15. Falling for Scams and Fraudulent Schemes

Many investors lose money to Ponzi schemes, unregulated brokers, and fraudulent opportunities.

How to Avoid:

Verify credentials of brokers and platforms with SEBI or other regulatory authorities.

Avoid schemes promising guaranteed, high, or risk-free returns.

Example: Always research and verify before investing in a "too good to be true" scheme promoted via social media.

16. Ignoring Diversification Across Geographies

Many investors focus solely on domestic investments, missing out on global opportunities.

How to Avoid:

Include international mutual funds or ETFs to gain exposure to global markets.

Diversify across sectors and geographies to reduce dependency on a single economy.

Example: Investing in US-based ETFs provides exposure to companies like Apple, Google, and Amazon, complementing domestic equity holdings.

Conclusion

Investing mistakes are inevitable but can be minimized with knowledge, planning, and discipline. Recognizing these pitfalls and implementing strategies to avoid them ensures a smoother path to wealth creation.

By focusing on informed decision-making, goal alignment, and consistent reviews, you can achieve financial stability and long-term success.

This chapter concludes our journey through the basics of the Indian stock market. Equipped with this knowledge, you're now ready to make informed decisions and embark on your investing journey with confidence.

NATIONAL STOCK EXCHANGE(NSE)

BOMBAY STOCK EXCHANGE (BSE)

HARSHAD MEHTA

BIG BULL

NASDAQ (THE US EXCHANGE)

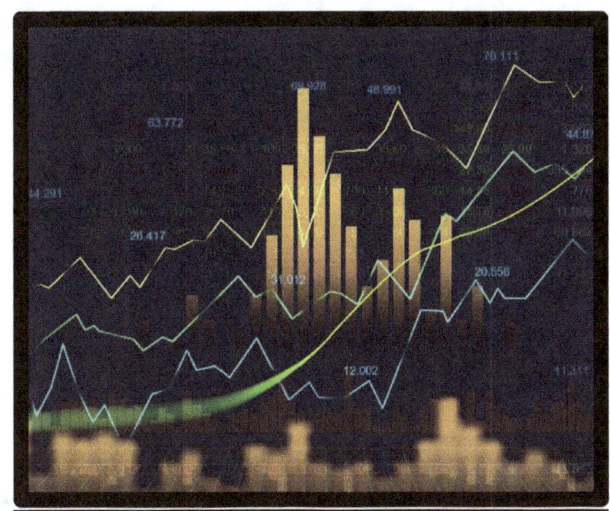

Stock Market Fell Flat, Sensex fell by more than 1000 points

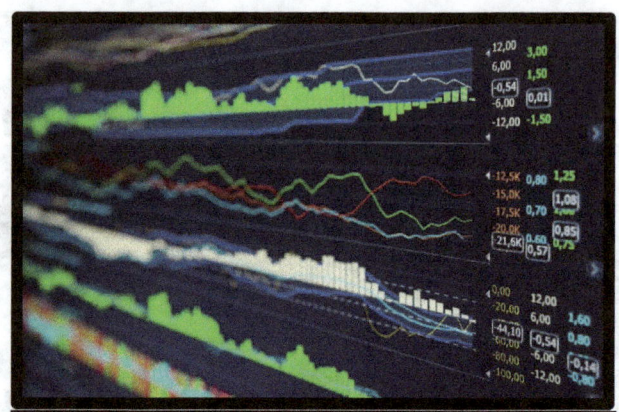

www.ingramcontent.com/pod-product-compliance
Lightning Source LLC
Chambersburg PA
CBHW071043240526
45471CB00014B/475